DOGS!

This Book Belongs to

_____

Interior and Cover Designer: Lisa Schreiber
Art Producer: Michael Hardgrove
Editor: Kristen Depken
Production Editor: Emily Sheehan

Illustrations: © 2019 Jake McDonald
Author photo courtesy of © Mark Deneen

ISBN: Print 978-1-64611-046-9

R0

DOGS!

A Coloring and Activity Book for Kids with Word Searches, Dot-to-Dots, Mazes, and More

Valerie Deneen

Illustrations by Jake McDonald

ROCKRIDGE
PRESS

Welcome to Dogs!

If you love dogs and enjoy coloring, this is the book for you! This book is filled with pictures to color and fun dog activities to do. You will learn lots of interesting facts about dogs and their training while doing word search puzzles, mazes, dot-to-dots, and more! You will also explore different dog breeds and learn more about the important jobs dogs do every day. The coloring pages can easily be torn out to give your unique coloring art to friends or family or to proudly display in your home. This book is sure to provide hours of dog-themed entertainment. Woof!

All About My Favorite Dog and Me:

My name is _____.

I am _____ years old.

I love dogs because _____.

If I had a dog, I would name it _____.

My favorite dog breed is _____
because _____.

Some activities I would do with my dog are

_____, _____,
and _____.

If my dog could talk, I would ask it _____.

My favorite place to take my dog would be _____
because _____.

My favorite book to read to my dog would be _____
by _____.

My dog's favorite treat would be _____.

Here is a drawing of my favorite dog:

Dog Tricks

Dogs can learn lots of tricks! Can you find all **7** words hidden in the puzzle below? Words are hidden three ways: from left to right, top to bottom, and diagonally from left to right.

FETCH   STAY   SIT

SHAKE   BARK   PLAY

              WAG

X F S P O K V L V B

F N G H D Z J H H F

D S K S S S X S Z K

D E T H W V N I B N

Z O F A X Y J T Y N

T E E K Y G F J I N

F I T E A Z A O P T

L W C W H O R S J B

A N H Y B A R K B D

X D V Y P L A Y C D

See pages 62–65 for the answer key!

This German shepherd is a police dog!

Find My Partner!

A police dog is also known as a K9. Help this K9 through the maze to find his partner at the end.

See pages 62–65 for the answer key!

Golden retrievers love to play catch!

Raise the Ruff!

Can you spot all **7** differences between these two doghouses?

See pages 62–65 for the answer key!

St. Bernards have made many mountain rescues!

Hungry Husky

This husky is looking for her food bowl!
Connect the dots so she can eat.

See pages 62–65 for the answer key!

Border collies are great at herding sheep!

At Your Service

Service dogs have very important jobs! Can you find all **6** words hidden in the puzzle below? Words are hidden three ways: from left to right, top to bottom, and diagonally from left to right.

TRAIN		SEARCH		RESCUE
POLICE		SLED		GUIDE

```
Z  S  S  Y  P  O  L  I  C  E
Z  Q  K  S  G  Y  K  X  D  G
Y  Q  V  E  M  Z  N  I  K  S
Q  T  R  A  I  N  U  D  E  L
T  Q  X  R  R  G  U  X  P  E
A  F  L  C  M  E  G  V  K  D
C  S  D  H  P  A  S  D  I  W
R  B  I  R  O  P  E  C  L  E
L  Y  B  V  Z  H  K  H  U  H
W  K  Q  E  C  T  F  Z  T  E
```

See pages 62–65 for the answer key!

Many firehouses adopt Dalmatians as mascots.

Wonderful Walks

Dogs love walks! Help this poodle find
his leash so he can go for a walk.

See pages 62–65 for the answer key!

Labrador retrievers are strong swimmers!

Spot the Difference

Dalmatians have lots of spots! Can you find all **6** differences between the patterns on these two Dalmatians?

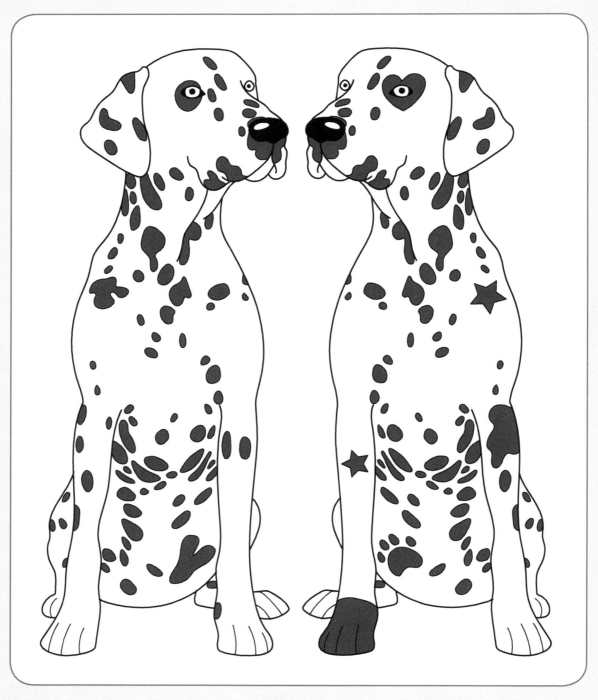

See pages 62–65 for the answer key!

The Chihuahua is the smallest breed of dog.

Cute Collar

This beagle is excited to get a new collar! Connect the dots to help put the collar on her.

See pages 62–65 for the answer key!

Pugs have wrinkly faces and curled tails!

Training Day

The words listed below are all used when training a dog. Can you find all **8** words hidden in the puzzle below? Words are hidden three ways: from left to right, top to bottom, and diagonally from left to right.

WALK	TREATS	JUMP
LEASH	TRICKS	WHISTLE
COLLAR	STAY	

```
T  T  S  J  X  Y  A  R  B  E
J  R  S  W  D  W  A  H  G  J
Y  I  E  W  A  L  K  A  E  R
R  C  H  A  L  E  N  Z  O  Y
I  K  Y  O  T  A  J  C  G  R
X  S  C  T  V  S  N  U  T  W
F  O  L  O  A  H  P  L  M  C
W  H  I  S  T  L  E  H  Y  P
J  F  T  S  T  A  Y  Z  P  L
L  J  O  R  E  V  B  V  G  U
```

See pages 62–65 for the answer key!

18

Dachshunds have short legs and long bodies!

19

Ready to Play!

This Jack Russell terrier loves to play!
Help her through the dog park maze below
to get to her ball at the end.

See pages 62–65 for the answer key!

This spitz has a new rope toy!

Cool Carriers

This bichon frise likes to travel in style! Can you find all **5** differences between his two pet carriers?

See pages 62–65 for the answer key!

Irish setters have long red fur. This one likes trail walks!

Last But Not Leashed

This cocker spaniel is ready for her leash! Connect the dots to give her a leash so she can go for a walk.

See pages 62–65 for the answer key!

This Rottweiler is being adopted at the animal shelter. Now he will have a new forever home!

Show Time!

Some dogs are trained to compete in shows! Can you find all **8** words hidden in the puzzle below? Words are hidden three ways: from left to right, top to bottom, and diagonally from left to right.

TRAINER	CONES	TRICKS
JUMP	ARENA	TUNNEL
PRIZE	RIBBON	

A	C	Y	L	A	Z	W	S	C	N
L	T	T	B	T	V	C	Q	N	E
T	R	N	M	Q	Y	O	H	U	N
A	A	S	K	K	E	J	U	M	P
T	I	B	A	R	E	N	A	C	C
U	N	R	P	R	I	Z	E	L	O
N	E	I	N	H	G	B	T	U	N
N	R	O	W	M	B	C	B	F	E
E	P	T	O	S	I	J	B	O	S
L	T	R	I	C	K	S	Y	F	N

See pages 62–65 for the answer key!

Mastiffs are very big. They are great guard dogs!

Precious Puppies

This Great Dane has lost her puppies!
Help her through the park maze to
reach her puppies at the end.

See pages 62–65 for the answer key!

Scottish terriers are also called Scotties. This Scottie loves his cozy sweater!

Grooming Gear

These French bulldogs are ready for a bath.
Can you spot all **6** differences during bath time?

See pages 62–65 for the answer key!

Pomeranians can be trained as medical alert dogs!

Rosette Ribbons

Many dog shows give ribbon awards to their winners. Dog show ribbons can have a rosette and hanging streamers. Connect the dots to give this Scottie his ribbon award.

See pages 62–65 for the answer key!

This shih tzu is competing in a dog show!

Dog Care

Caring for a dog can be a lot of hard work! Can you find all **8** words hidden in the puzzle below? Words are hidden three ways: from left to right, top to bottom, and diagonally from left to right.

FOOD	PLAY	WATER
WALK	HOME	GROOM
COLLAR	LEASH	

H L W R N V I E T F

L M V M R H O M E V

V E A F O O D C P R

M S A O Z P I W J C

P U F S G W D H D O

L U W D H O A P A L

A U D A F W L T S L

Y D E U L Y G G E A

R Y Z K K K L F G R

Z C G R O O M M R H

See pages 62–65 for the answer key!

This Australian shepherd jumps through hoops for his owner!

Show Time!

This corgi is competing in an agility show! Help him through the show maze to reach the ribbon at the end.

See pages 62–65 for the answer key!

This Siberian husky enjoys cold weather and hiking in the mountains!

Pooch Picnic

These two Yorkshire terriers are getting ready to go on a picnic with their owners! Can you spot all **6** differences between their travel gear below?

See pages 62–65 for the answer key!

Mexican hairless dogs are also known as Xolos.

Puppy Bedtime

This Boston terrier puppy is feeling sleepy after a day at the dog park! Connect the dots to make a cozy dog bed so she can rest.

See pages 62–65 for the answer key!

This coonhound puppy loves to play outside!

Snow Dog

Sled dogs enjoy playing in snow and cold weather!
Can you find all **8** words hidden in the puzzle below?
Words are hidden three ways: from left to right, top
to bottom, and diagonally from left to right.

SNOW	PULL	RACE
DELIVER	STRONG	ICE
MOVE	ARCTIC	

```
X  G  H  E  L  R  N  H  G  F
N  R  B  G  W  J  B  M  O  D
S  T  R  O  N  G  G  A  E  S
G  F  Y  X  L  S  N  R  D  Q
Z  S  G  P  U  L  L  C  E  K
D  N  F  I  J  T  E  T  L  X
S  O  I  C  F  V  V  I  I  J
L  W  O  E  O  K  V  C  V  N
U  C  S  M  W  R  A  C  E  F
V  H  T  D  I  K  H  A  R  W
```

See pages 62–65 for the answer key!

This basset hound is celebrating his Gotcha Day, or the day he was adopted by his family!

Water Park

Dogs need to drink fresh water every day!
Help this basset hound through the park maze
to get to the dog water fountain at the end.

See pages 62–65 for the answer key!

Jack Russell terriers
can be trained to act for
television and movies!

Just Fur Fun!

These two poodle puppies are back from the groomers.
Can you spot all **6** differences between the images?

See pages 62–65 for the answer key!

The bichon frise is fluffy, white, and very cuddly!

In the Doghouse

This boxer dog spends a lot of time playing outside in the yard. Connect the dots to make a doghouse so he has a place to rest and relax.

See pages 62–65 for the answer key!

This cocker spaniel loves to play in piles of leaves!

Furever Useful

Dogs can have many important jobs! Can you find all **7** words hidden in the puzzle below? Words are hidden three ways: from left to right, top to bottom, and diagonally from left to right.

ACTING   RESCUE   POLICE

THERAPY   GUIDE   HERD

                   SEARCH

Y J T H E R A P Y D

G R F D S E A R C H

L Z I C S C L G A C

B U J M D Z Z P L S

G K Q T C K U O H O

Q H G Q P Y Y L U Y

P A C T I N G I Q U

N R E S C U E C F U

M M O J D R S E L S

R E H E R D L H M K

See pages 62–65 for the answer key!

This Great Dane wants to play fetch!

Doggie Paddle

This Labrador retriever loves to swim for her ball!
Can you help her swim through the maze below
to get to her tennis ball at the end?

See pages 62–65 for the answer key!

This French bulldog is cooling off in the pool on a hot summer day.

Tricky Toys

These two Irish setters love to play with their toys! Can you spot all **5** differences between their toys shown below?

See pages 62–65 for the answer key!

This corgi likes to run through fields of flowers!

Ruffreshing Treat

This Boston terrier would love to eat some dog ice cream! Can you connect the dots to give her a special cool treat?

See pages 62–65 for the answer key!

This Yorkshire terrier gets lots of exercise playing fetch with his tennis ball.

Hot Diggity Dog

Dogs that get too much sun can get a sunburn! Can you help this Xolo puppy through the sunny beach maze below to get to the shady umbrella at the end?

See pages 62–65 for the answer key!

This whippet is playing flyball!
Flyball is an exciting relay race
with hurdles and a tennis ball.

Countless Canines

There are many different dog breeds! Can you find all **7** words hidden in the puzzle below? Words are hidden three ways: from left to right, top to bottom, and diagonally from left to right.

BEAGLE   SHELTIE   PUG

SPITZ   POODLE   CORGI

                BOXER

```
D  X  J  Y  R  X  P  U  G  C
E  S  H  E  L  T  I  E  A  X
Q  S  E  Q  I  J  B  X  S  F
B  E  A  G  L  E  P  K  K  Q
K  V  R  R  D  S  W  D  C  P
F  O  X  S  P  I  T  Z  P  O
C  F  B  O  X  E  R  S  T  O
K  Y  Z  Y  V  X  R  L  M  D
H  C  P  I  Y  W  P  R  A  L
N  E  Y  X  U  D  O  V  G  E
```

See pages 62–65 for the answer key!

**Papillon dogs are famous
for having ears that look
like butterfly wings!**

Answer Key

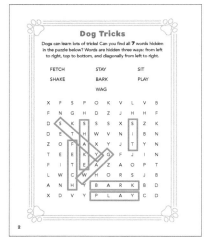

Dog Tricks

Dogs can learn lots of tricks! Can you find all **7** words hidden in the puzzle below? Words are hidden three ways: from left to right, top to bottom, and diagonally from left to right.

FETCH   STAY   SIT
SHAKE   BARK   PLAY
WAG

2

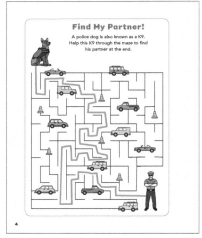

Find My Partner!

A police dog is also known as a K9. Help this K9 through the maze to find his partner at the end.

4

Raise the Ruff!

Can you spot all **7** differences between these two doghouses?

6

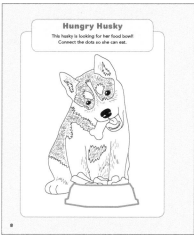

Hungry Husky

This husky is looking for her food bowl! Connect the dots so she can eat.

8

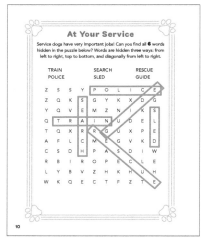

At Your Service

Service dogs have very important jobs! Can you find all **6** words hidden in the puzzle below? Words are hidden three ways: from left to right, top to bottom, and diagonally from left to right.

TRAIN   SEARCH   RESCUE
POLICE   SLED   GUIDE

10

Wonderful Walks

Dogs love walks! Help this poodle find his leash so he can go for a walk.

12

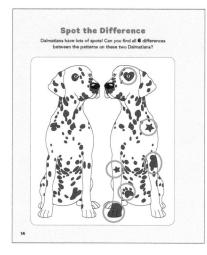

Spot the Difference

Dalmatians have lots of spots! Can you find all **6** differences between the patterns on these two Dalmatians?

14

Cute Collar

This beagle is excited to get a new collar! Connect the dots to help put the collar on her.

16

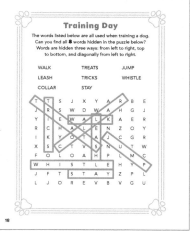

Training Day

The words listed below are all used when training a dog. Can you find all **8** words hidden in the puzzle below? Words are hidden three ways: from left to right, top to bottom, and diagonally from left to right.

WALK   TREATS   JUMP
LEASH   TRICKS   WHISTLE
COLLAR   STAY

18

Ready to Play!

This Jack Russell terrier loves to play! Help her through the dog park maze below to get to her ball at the end.

20

Cool Carriers

This bichon frise likes to travel in style! Can you find all **5** differences between his two pet carriers?

22

Last But Not Leashed

This cocker spaniel is ready for her leash! Connect the dots to give her a leash so she can go for a walk.

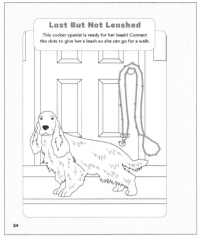

24

Show Time!

Some dogs are trained to compete in shows! Can you find all **8** words hidden in the puzzle below? Words are hidden three ways: from left to right, top to bottom, and diagonally from left to right.

TRAINER   CONES   TRICKS
JUMP   ARENA   TUNNEL
PRIZE   RIBBON

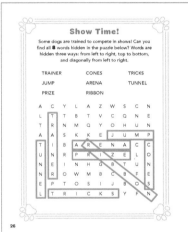

26

Precious Puppies

This Great Dane has lost her puppies! Help her through the park maze to reach her puppies at the end.

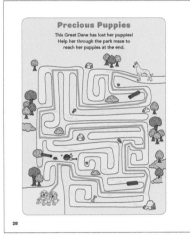

28

Grooming Gear

These French bulldogs are ready for a bath. Can you spot all **6** differences during bath time?

30

Rosette Ribbons

Many dog shows give ribbon awards to their winners. Dog show ribbons can have a rosette and hanging streamers. Connect the dots to give this Scottie his ribbon award.

32

Dog Care

Caring for a dog can be a lot of hard work! Can you find all **8** words hidden in the puzzle below? Words are hidden three ways: from left to right, top to bottom, and diagonally from left to right.

FOOD   PLAY   WATER
WALK   HOME   GROOM
COLLAR   LEASH

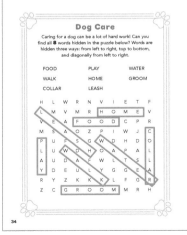

34

Show Time!

This corgi is competing in an agility show! Help him through the show maze to reach the ribbon at the end.

36

63

Answer Key

Pooch Picnic

These two Yorkshire terriers are getting ready to go on a picnic with their owners! Can you spot all **6** differences between their travel gear below?

38

Puppy Bedtime

This Boston terrier puppy is feeling sleepy after a day at the dog park! Connect the dots to make a cozy dog bed so she can rest.

40

Snow Dog

Sled dogs enjoy playing in snow and cold weather! Can you find all **8** words hidden in the puzzle below? Words are hidden three ways: from left to right, top to bottom, and diagonally from left to right.

SNOW   PULL   RACE
DELIVER   STRONG   ICE
MOVE   ARCTIC

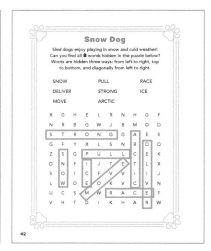

42

Water Park

Dogs need to drink fresh water every day! Help this basset hound through the park maze to get to the dog water fountain at the end.

44

Just Fur Fun!

These two poodle puppies are back from the groomers. Can you spot all **6** differences between the images?

46

In the Doghouse

This boxer dog spends a lot of time playing outside in the yard. Connect the dots to make a doghouse so he has a place to rest and relax.

48

Furever Useful

Dogs can have many important jobs! Can you find all **7** words hidden in the puzzle below? Words are hidden three ways: from left to right, top to bottom, and diagonally from left to right.

ACTING   RESCUE   POLICE
THERAPY   GUIDE   HERD
SEARCH

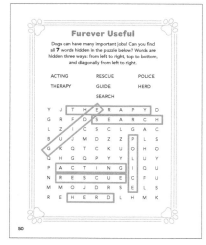

50

Doggie Paddle

This Labrador retriever loves to swim for her ball! Can you help her swim through the maze below to get to her tennis ball at the end?

52

Tricky Toys

These two Irish setters love to play with their toys! Can you spot all **5** differences between their toys shown below?

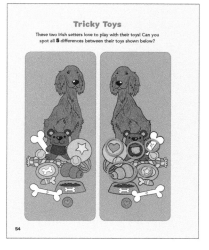

54

64

Ruffreshing Treat

This Boston terrier would love to eat some dog ice cream! Can you connect the dots to give her a special cool treat?

56

Hot Diggity Dog

Dogs that get too much sun can get a sunburn! Can you help this Xolo puppy through the sunny beach maze below to get to the shady umbrella at the end?

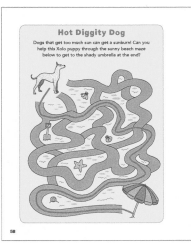

58

Countless Canines

There are many different dog breeds! Can you find all **7** words hidden in the puzzle below? Words are hidden three ways: from left to right, top to bottom, and diagonally from left to right.

BEAGLE   SHELTIE   PUG

SPITZ   POODLE   CORGI

BOXER

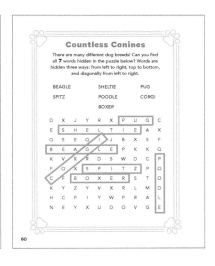

D X J Y R X P U G C
E S H E L T I E A X
Q S E Q I J B X S F
B E A G L E P K K Q
K V R R D S W D C P
F O X S P I T Z P O
C F B O X E R S T O
K Y Z Y V X R L M D
H C P I Y W P R A L
N E Y X U D O V G E

60

About the Author

Valerie Deneen is the founder of InnerChildFun.com, where she writes about what to do with kids, creative play for all ages, parenting tips and tricks, learning and educational activities for kids, craft ideas for tweens  and school-aged children, and gardening with kids. Valerie is a speaker, creative play advocate, brand ambassador, television personality, and active Rotarian. Her work has been featured in *Highlights High Five*, *FamilyFun Magazine*, *PBS Parents*, various morning talk shows, and several online publications. For creative play ideas sent directly to your inbox, visit Valerie's blog at InnerChildFun.com and subscribe to the weekly newsletter.

CPSIA information can be obtained
at www.ICGtesting.com
Printed in the USA
JSHW040735060420
4971JS00001B/1